GW01606488

Miles of Sky Above Us,
Miles of Earth Below

Steve Denehan

For my family and friends and for James, for taking a chance.

Cover Painting by Steve Denehan

Printed in the U.S.A.
Published by **Cajun Mutt Press**

Table of Contents:

Table of Contents:

Table of Contents:

Jesus or Rasputin

I wonder how many times have these raindrops fallen
they land on the attic window
loud and heavy
reminding us that eventually
they will win

I wonder what these raindrops have fallen on
spitfires and lollipops
brides and widows
endings, beginnings
endings

I wonder if these raindrops have fallen
on Hitler or Harold Lloyd
Cleopatra or Elvis
you
Jesus
or Rasputin

the sky is a grey lake
pouring itself upon us
muddying the garden
puddling the drive
trapping us, again
it is June

Ivory

The ceiling was wallpapered with a tropical scene
there were palm trees with heavy leaves
a flamingo standing, one-legged, in blue shallows
water that I knew to be warm
a flamingo oblivious to my discomfort
oblivious to the man beneath him
trying desperately to pull a tooth from my mouth

he had the tooth clamped in some sort of dental pliers
he pushed and pulled and tried to be gentle
he had said that it would be quick
but minutes were passing
small talk had stopped
his brow was pursed
I could tell that he was trying not to grunt

he had told me that it would be painless
to raise my hand if I felt something
anything
first of all, I felt pressure
I felt the weight of him push onto my jaw
I heard, I felt, the sound of metal on ivory
cracks and creaks finding their way to my ear
by dancing along my jawbone

then, like a train in the distance
announcing itself on tracks of bone
there was pain, snaking its way toward me
I don't know why
but I decided to test myself
instead of raising my hands
I put them deep in my pockets
balled them into fists and waited

I didn't have to wait long
it came, hot and loud and I told myself
to hold on, that it would be over soon

I felt sweat bloom on my forehead
I saw purple flowers above me
as he pulled and twisted
the dizzying metallic taste of blood reached my throat
and I clenched my fists and begged myself to see it through

the train rattled through me and I swear I could hear its whistle
a screaming white noise in my skull
and then it was gone
and the world started turning again
and he held my tooth before me
proud, like a big game hunter
and over his shoulder I glimpsed the flamingo
turning away from me in disgust

Eye Chart

1.

The blade was slight and pure
his hand, mercifully, was steady
I was still as my stomach leaped
I think I heard it
the sound of the slicing
of my cornea

I didn't see it as I was blind
temporarily at least
unblinking
my eyelids held open by a tool
a tiny forceps
a speculum he called it

thin layers were removed from my cornea
with, almost impossibly
a laser
I tried to be still
as suddenly
every part of me thrummed

2.

she sat in the chair
made higher for little girls
her brow furrowed as she read the eye chart
easy at first but soon
she stumbled
once, and then again

the optician replaced the chart
my little girl
in the high chair
still, with furrowed brow
tried again

and stumbled, and stumbled

the optician handed her a pair of glasses
she put them on
instantly, jarringly older
and smiled
and read
effortlessly, all the way to the bottom

3.

we watched her play with the toys
tongue peeking out of the corner of her half-smile
she couldn't hear us
couldn't hear that it was window glass in the frames
couldn't know how even her lie
could make my heart laugh

My Father Was a Carpenter

We used to sharpen sticks together
sitting in front of pastel sunsets
cloaked in birdsong
he, imparting secret wisdom
while yellow wood shavings pooled between our feet
it would take a while
a long while sometimes
to get the points just right

we would watch them arc across the sky
and I remember worrying
about low flying planes
and how his laugh would startle watching birds
how our spears would land
just right, sometimes
the point buried in the soil beneath
his, suddenly, imperfect lawn

I watched a program yesterday
there is a machine
that can sharpen pieces of dowel
dozens and dozens of wooden dowels
simultaneously
in a matter of seconds
before they are deposited
mechanically
into a huge container
their points are perfect
clean
and sharp
so very sharp

Casual Fridays

I worked for an insurance company
where we worked to convince the vulnerable
to bet against themselves

behind the scenes morale was wilting
smiles were pained and strained
souls and hearts were stained

the bigwigs met
talked about how to raise morale
a happy worker is a good worker
we were summoned and they announced
Casual Fridays

I sat at my desk one Friday afternoon
looked around the office
at everyone dressed in their casual clothes
even the bigwigs
rendering them more human
supposedly, and yet
I hated them
and myself
just the same

months passed and we were summoned again
there were to be no more Casual Fridays
somehow, they had decided
morale was now too high

I cleared my throat to speak
then thought the better of it

Stairs

The towel came soft and warm from the tumble dryer
she sat in her vest
her mouth full of cereal
the spoon heavy with more
watching her program
eyes wide and hungry

I draped the towel across her shoulders
she purred and cloaked it around her
instantly, magically warm
safe
"Did your Mam do this to you when you were small Dad?"

I am standing on the stairs
halfway up
I slip
tumble silently
arrive in my childhood
see my mother walking toward me
arms wide
a towel stretched between them
waiting for me

"She did, and maybe you can do the same for your children."
she is silent
her mouth full of cereal
the spoon heavy with more
watching her program
eyes wide and hungry

she speaks again, her words clouded with munching
"But who will wrap a warm towel around you now Dad?"
I smile and kiss her cheek
it is enough

there are no more warm towels for me
but there are blackbirds

cobwebs twinkling in sun showers
the smell of coffee
Tom Waits in the morning
The Blue Nile in the evening
and her
more than enough

Black Cadillac

I woke into a grey and heavy room
the legacy of a dream

the hustle bustle morning came
went
we drove the back roads
snaked around the bends
bounced over undulations
arrived

she did not step outside to meet us
not this time
she looked unsure
unsteady
we sat
danced around it for a while

the grey and heavy slipped under the door
her smile fell away
she meekly announced a most unwelcome visitor
a tumour, large and hard, on her leg

cancer
always cancer

we danced again
"stay positive"
"fingers crossed"
"they can do great things now"
danced our way to the car
and drove

and who knows
they *can* do great things now
and she might see us all off
might make it to the end
die *with* her cancer

not because of it

in my dream Death drove a Cadillac
black of course
a cue ball gearstick
furry dice swinging from the rear-view mirror
a speck on the horizon
but from the look of plumes of dust
driving hard
with room enough for all of us

Idle Threats and Patios

His weight loss
sudden and dramatic
rendered him taller
an illusion

before his smile
wide and hopeless
rendered him smaller

we sat on the patio
pretending that things were okay
that the bag of clothes in the boot of his car
was an idle threat
just for show
to show her
to show himself
we talked

like we used to
before idle threats and patios
we talked
like we never had
of his future
a future that sat with us
laughing softly

midnight slipped by
the sky heavy
we reminisced
were young again
he stood to leave
the spare room was his but
he didn't want it
not then

his tail lights dazzled at first
before being taken by the dark

he, and his bag of clothes, were gone
I rinsed his glass and locked up
suddenly tired

Verdant

We stared at the lava lamp
talked a while
listened to the airplanes take off
land
thirty-five years passed
things were the same
things were different

despite it all
the discouragement
the tutting
head shaking
the criticism
the silence
despite it all
I was writing

reading too
and sick
and tired
of poems about love
and self-loathing
and nature
the sky is blue
just like your soul
we get it

verdant no more
cerulean no more
obsidian no more
enough
enough
enough

give me poems of bile and blood
of finding his toenail clippings under the skirting board
years after

of the scar on her forehead
and the blood on his bed
of the walls and the wails
and the bitten down nails
give me sweat, skin and bone
and an unanswered phone
make it real
give me real
give me real

The Barman

I thought I had it pretty much figured out
until I sat here
at this dusty bar
lit by the oh-so eager eyes
and dazzling smile of the barman

I had cultivated a simple life-philosophy
follow our cat's lead and aim low
looking only to find that perfect square of sun
to stretch out and lie in
and watch the rest blur past
in a whirr of stern brows and small screens

then I was corrected by this barman
this man of glints and twinkles and surely that glass is dry now
and can't he see that I am not that guy
that I am not ripe for his life lessons
that I came in here to escape
to be left alone
to *hide* from glints and twinkles

on and on he goes
curling my toes and turning my stomach
with his reconstituted platitudes
and practised whimsy
with his air quotes misuse
and third person overuse
and I look away
to see an empty whiskey glass to my left

my life is yellow teeth
and yellow pages
and yellow blood through my yellow heart
but there is a fly at the bottom of the glass
six legs up
worse off than me
or so I think

he twitches, slowly at first
and the barman's words become those of a man
who has fallen through a manhole
the fly jitters to its feet and I am with him
I watch him steady himself
I imagine the fire in him, unbridled
how he will return to the other flies a god
how he will regale them with his stories
while feasting on a piece of rotten apple
how he will die another day but live on in legend
the drone of the barman is suddenly replaced by the drone of wings
the fly is airborne
as am I
I stand and watch, unblinking
this most glorious of operas
he flies right by my eyes
a wounded spitfire sputtering heroically
I watch him aim for the window
for balmy autumn breezes and car horns and a second chance

I watch him hit the windowpane and fall pathetically
landing on the sill
six legs up again
I sit back down
maybe he will rise again

Shoulders

There were dozens of small paintings on the wall
paintings all the way from South Africa
the waiter had said, excitedly
though they must have been wallpaper to him by now

I could feel her eyes beckoning me from the top of the restaurant
my father stood beside her, head bowed and cocked slightly

I reached him and put my hand on his back
he still had his coat on, the coldness never leaving him now
he held his credit card in his hand and stared at it
as if it were new to him
or a puzzle, impossible to decipher
"It's okay, Dad."

I gave my card and waited, watching him shuffle from us
his face expressionless, his body deflated
I kept my eyes on him as I was sure if I looked away
he would step into a bottomless puddle and be gone
I noticed the narrow slope of his shoulders
shoulders where once I perched, giggling
my stomach doing loop-the-loops
one hundred feet in the air

he sat at the table, still holding the credit card
in his old carpenter's hands
I rested my hand on his back again
silently pleading with him
to forgive himself
"I forgot my pin number."
"I know, Dad."
"I hate it."

the silence was water
seeping slowly through our clothes
waking me
I pointed upward

“Those paintings come all the way from South Africa, Dad.”.
he pulled his eyes from the credit card and said
“That one looks like an angel.”

Recent Experience with a Publisher

Apathy
a small word
though it holds so much

paranoia, despair and hopelessness
peek out
from between the letters

behind it lurks anger
smouldering
ready to
but never quite
catching fire

beneath it
a foundation of eggshells
and broken glass sneers

and above it
the last shreds of my self

respect and esteem
evaporating
into a laughing
sunless
sky

A Moment

His face is covered though I can see his eyes
they are without sympathy
this is as it should be
I try to keep my voice steady
"Can you tell me when?
When the moment has arrived?"
he owes me nothing
he says, "yes"

I am to be the last man guillotined in France
the thoughts in my head are many and many coloured
though swirled together they make a grey
I can hear my heart, its last few beats are loud
it is making them count
I allow myself to be scared
he says
"this is the moment"
it is a long moment, it stretches
and then

The Sign on the Side of a Pub in Prosperous, County Kildare

We pass it by most days
the sign
"Spooktacular Halloween Party Tonight!"
it is hanging since 2016
when my daughter, 7 years-old now
"was young"

we pass it by most days
laughing
"Can we go, Dad?"
        "What will you dress as?"
"A zombie mermaid."
        "Of course!"

the sign says
"Spot Prizes!"
my daughter says
"I wonder what the spot prizes were, Dad."
        "What do you think they were?"
"Maybe a lovely picture in a frame."
"Or a purse with jewels."
"Or a puppy."

whatever they might have been
I am sure
that they are long forgotten now

Quaker Village

As we drive the snow comes down hard and soft
just the day before I had learned of a Quaker village
mired within this Catholic place
we park our nondescript car and dissolve
into our surroundings

the subject has made bad decisions
we wait and watch for him
should he appear we are to follow
we wait
minutes become hours
we go for a walk to stretch our legs
still watching

the Quaker village is silent under snow
our breath is smoke in the air
as we talk the sound is flat, the musicality taken
the sky is a melted pearl
it could be morning, or evening
it is in between

I know that nothing will happen
I know that our subject will not move
not today, this day of snow but
I imagine him emerging, unable to resist the whiteness, the
softness, the purity
I imagine him seeing us, catching eyes with me for a slow
moment
I see his hand reach inside his coat
I see the matte black finish of a gun

against the snow, it is as black as anything, as everything
there is no echo
the sound is dead, flat, loud
I see the pearly sky and feel the cold around me, seeping inward
I wish I could see the dark red flowing into the snow
I imagine it would be beautiful

Dublin Airport

I grew up near the airport
a boy in awe of metal giants
their screaming underbellies inching
across coloured canvas skies
just beyond my reach

soft droning lullabies passed by my bedroom window
I slept to them
I woke to them
I lay in summer grass
watching their vapour trails pattern the blue
and

waved
I always waved
in my mother's arms
looking up
waving madly
on my tricycle
my bicycle
looking up
waving madly

we visited the airport
on lucky Sunday afternoons
there were arcade machines there
for 10p I was a barbarian
a ninja, a knight
for 10p
I was someone else

we would watch the planes from the viewing gallery
impossibly huge, almost prehistoric
their rivets gleaming
the pilots settling into the cockpits
as if it were not a magical thing

the hostesses would walk past
would sometimes smile
would bring heartbeats thumping to my ears
would leave exotic perfumes behind
that I would hold in my lungs
and breathe out again as a gasp

I waved and waved and wondered
whether they could see me
whether they might be waving back
whether we might meet someday
and somehow, halfway know

I was a boy that grew up near the airport
then a man
a man who no longer waved
a man who finally walked up the steps
who took his seat in the fuselage
who waited
to fly away

the pilot spoke
the seatbelts clicked
the engine roared
we left the world behind
with, once again
heartbeats thumping in my ears

I looked down to see toy cars
on toy roads
weaving through toy countryside
I saw my home ahead
I saw my mother hanging clothes
I knew that she would have clothes pegs between her teeth
I noticed my hand waving
as if on autopilot
but she did not look up
and then was gone
and so was I

September Book Launch (Written in May)

I consider the size of my life
am I The Eiffel Tower
the Golden Gate Bridge
a shopping mall
a fast food drive thru
the local pet shop
a two-bed semi
a toilet cubicle
if even

regardless, a book launch looms
September, dreaded once
as the end of summer
and start of school
now ominous once again

I imagine sinking low into a chair
slowly, like a submarine
wishing to sink further
beneath the table
through the sticky vinyl flooring

I imagine the murmured silence as I walk to the rostrum
invisible broken glass crunching beneath me
slicing in to me

to dispense pieces of myself
to a half empty room

at best
at worst

The Summer Blurs by Outside

The sun shines above us
inside us
we walk through Newbridge
her hand still small in mine
the metre of her voice questioning
or joyous exclamation

we had aimed to be aimless
and fill the day with beautiful, easy nothings
I watch her look
I watch her see
her hand still small in mine
but growing, gently growing

we drive home with the windows open
the summer blurs by outside
"Why is it called Newbridge, Dad? It looks old."
        "It was new once."
"Like you!"
like me

Two Steps Forward, Two Steps Back

These days are not yet memories
but soon
they will be
and soon after that
they won't

we are told to keep moving forward
but who are they to tell us
and who are we to listen
it is okay to stay put
or move backward

as long
as we remember
that we
for the most part
get what we deserve

Somewhereanywhere

I'm getting close now
close to standing up
to begin
something
anything

I'm getting close now
close to stamping my feet
to hear
to feel
somethinganything

I'm getting close now
close to running
away, away
to, to
somewhereanywhere

I stand
I stamp
I run
to the bathroom
I shave off my beard
watch it fall into the sink

broken shadows

I am still underneath

Zach Gassman

I buy old library books
because they are cheap
because they come with extras
history
stories beyond the books themselves

I am reading one now by a long-gone poet
one of my guys
written in his later years
when he was comfortable
coasting
the venom in him much less potent

it had been checked out just once
from Elkhart Public Library, Indiana
by Zach Gassman, who had used an old bank statement for a bookmark

on the 20th of May 2001
the Twin Towers' last summer
his teller had been Bobby
and there was $7.04 in his account

I am here to type these words
I hope that he is there
somewhere
to read them

alive and well
dead and gone
I don't know

what I do know
is that that summer
he had the sum total of $7.04 in his account
I hope he spent it foolishly

Phantom Limb Syndrome

I worked for a private detective agency
we were hired by insurance companies
to investigate false accident claims

we would be sent to place people
"subjects"
under surveillance
to ensure that their payments
received as a result of accident
or illness
were still required

we were hired to surveil a man
a rally driving fanatic
who had attended a race
who had stood too close to the road
to the cars
who had been hit
and lost his arm

an instant amputee
agony
multiple operations
years of recovery
and adaptation
now, phantom limb syndrome
and pity

we waited at the clinic
watched him arrive for his check-up
he wore a rally driving jacket
I thought, that's real love

one of the sleeves was empty
it hadn't grown back
he still had no arm
was still an amputee

disabled

the company made €1,800 for that
good money even now

Hate

My father would tell me
that I didn't really mean it
no doubt dismayed at how his son
a boy with the whole world around him
could use the word *hate*
so casually

he would put his hands on my narrow shoulders
look down at my upturned face
and insist that I didn't really hate
that there was no room in the world
in me
for hate

I hate
that he was wrong

The Tragedy of the One-Armed Man

For twenty years he
tall and lean
has wandered through the town
head down
one arm searching for litter
and a swaying, empty sleeve
marking the absence of the other

I wonder about him
about his family
maybe he has none
maybe he
or they
pulled away
maybe he prefers his own company

but
there has got to be something more than picking up
after the worst of us
I have looked in vain for the honour in it
the dignity
the spirituality in it
watched for twenty years him struggle
to push his cart on weathering paths
invisible

as if it was somehow infused with meaning
one good arm
wasted
an arm that could caress her
write to him
comfort them
if given the chance

instead
he walks into the cold
his sleeve blowing behind him

pointing at what might have been

corner boys casually scatter empty crisp packets
and flick cigarette butts
killing him slowly
from a distance
or

maybe it is a mercy
an unmeant kindness
providing him with purpose
in the absence of everything
of anything else
either way
the wind is cold tonight and plays
with cans and plastic bags
before dropping them in gutters
at the playground gate
and they wait for him
just as he waits for them

he squints and hunts
finds and discards
plastic cups, crumpled cans
and time
and maybe his name
someday
will be etched on a plaque
when he has been forgotten
while in the town, they will wonder
why, suddenly
there is litter all around

Several Fields Over

Her voice is on the breeze
a distant softness
talking, sometimes singing
several fields over
we have never met
she, a blur
a stranger
to me

but
I have heard her sing to herself
I have heard her call her children
out of the rain
into the sun
I have heard her berate and chide
and laugh

like the lowing of the cows
the whisper of the grass
the buzzing flies and chirping birds
her voice is there
stitched into the fabric of the air
yet

if we were to meet, I suspect
knowing myself as I do
I would not like her
would want to get away from her
and she from me

she is out there
a few fields away
hanging her clothes
wishing away the rain
and that
for both of us
is enough

Sports Day

I wake into a morning, golden, and shimmering with summer dew
I hear her voice outside, giddy, swirling, music to me
I drag my own, dry as chalk, up from my stomach, and open the window
"Hello Robin!"
        "Hi Dad! You sound croaky! You sound old!"
"I *am* old!"
        "No you're not! Not yet!"

today is her sports day and the only thing interrupting the blue
is the singing yellow sun
we were promised rain
never trust the weatherman

she wears socks with little capes
they make her go faster she tells me
though I think she knows
deep down
it not to be true
I can't wait to watch her

the rest run to win, their little faces determined, grimacing
the child falling from them
she runs to be free, smiling, curls straightening behind her
capes flapping at her ankles
and I am on her shoulder
whispering my love in giggles to her

she collects her medals and puts them in her pocket
she says that she doesn't want to show off
my heart, my heart, my heart
we go for ice cream to celebrate
he overhears us talking about the sports day
and makes hers extra tall
with extra syrup, lime
because we have never tasted lime syrup before
tang on our tongues

ice cream smiles

on the way home I hear on the radio that on average
151,600 people die every day
I look in the rear-view mirror
her half-gone ice cream in her hand
she is steaming up her window
and drawing stars and rainbows

Nothing Is Remembered

We dine in the shadow of a building
a monument of impossibility
a building of no corners
of unexpected curves and twists
as if the concrete had been poured into an enormous, intricate mould
then left to set for one hundred years

we watch it come alive in the setting sun
sounds wash over us
the soft screech of cutlery
the always urgent Catalan tongues
the perpetual whine of moped engines
an infinite river of moped engines

I gaze at this building, slowly melting in dwindling light
I hear the sounds grow silent, as if the sun is snow, dampening them
I do not blink and for a time it is just it
and me and nothing else
the world has fallen away
it is a perfect moment
maybe the only perfect moment
yet I know
eventually
it will be forgotten

The Heartbeats of a Tadpole

We walked through the stream
ankle deep in the narrow shallows
feeling the weight and cool of the water
push against our wellington boots

once, the water ran clear
as it listened, twinkling
to my swooping, joyous childhood
once, it teemed with tadpoles
pinkeens, sticklebacks

now, the shimmer has dulled
the twinkles fight against the oil
the grease and the scum
some still make it through
but the stream is dead

then
a shriek
and she is away
her net in the air
the sun, her hair
she tramples though the stream
and I follow
splash for splash
"a tadpole dad!"
"a tadpole!"

we charge after it
the stream jumps into my boots
that coldness
that strange intimacy
"my socks are wet dad!"
          "it doesn't matter, keep running!"
never ever stop running

today, the first of December
I sit here, inside
safe
warm
far from streams
reminiscing
I remember her stopping
turning to me
wet to her knees
her face had fallen
“please don’t be sad dad.”
          “why would I be sad?”
“he has escaped
I couldn’t catch him
but that’s okay
I didn’t want to catch him
not really
tadpoles are alive too.”

Knuckles Bruised from Punching Raindrops

I sit here trying to write
trying not to listen
but hearing
a car alarm, distant
relentless

it woke me this morning
bleeding into my dream
dragging me into Monday
it has been hours now
Jesus Christ

I remain calm
I try to remain calm
but the words are there inside my fingertips
eager to be born
trapped

I woke to sunlight
now it rains and I imagine
my throat hot and raw from screaming at the sun
my knuckles bruised from punching raindrops
I go into the garden

look toward the sound
consider the possibility that it could be in my head
that I have woken up changed, mad
the alarm gets louder
comes closer

and perches on our washing line
a car alarm
in the throat
of a blackbird
Jesus
Christ

in the absence of a flamethrower
I clap my hands and watch
the car-alarm-bird fly
in silence, towards the city
and I am not insane, not yet

Joseph Merrick

We are the elephants
the ones who could not
would not
forget

130 years after you left us
suffocated by yourself at 27
we found you
we found you

a lifetime of torment was not enough
not for us
we made you an exhibit in life
now in death

you lay
and were found
in the City of London Cemetery
beside Jack the Ripper's victims
and other broken people
happily forgotten
in quiet, unmarked graves

you have known what it is
to be pointed at
run toward
run from
you must have known
that we would not rest
as you have tried to
that we would find you
resurrect you
as a new Lazarus so
we can point again

we will not lose you this time
we will keep you safe

a curiosity
an exhibit once again
and all the dead unborn
and all the unborn dead
will know you

will think they know you

All Damn Morning

It's been at it all damn morning
scurrying, tapping, hammering
something small
a rodent
a bird
panicked
relentless

it's been moving along the outside edge of the house
back and forth
forth and back
eventually, I drag the old, folding ladder
open it and get a shot of liquid cold
sour rusty water
up my sleeve

"it" isn't in the gutter so I traipse up to the attic
balancing on beams in creaking light
listening, looking for movement in the shadows
nothing, of course

I potter in the kitchen
waiting for the next flurry of sound in the eves
wondering if the rodent or bird can hear me
if it is curious at all
or so consumed by fear that all it hears
are white and furious heartbeats

there is nothing I can do now
but wait
wait and pretend not to notice the slowing
of the scurrying, tapping, hammering
pretend not to know that someday
I will be in the eves
and someone else will be waiting
and pretending

Christmas Morning

I listened to her clamber out of bed
excitement in her little feet
her eyes so wide I saw the whites of them
across our waking bedroom

we ran to the sitting room, all of us
then, we stood back
as she opened the door
with a caution so earnest

a gasp and a squeal and her arms to the sky
Santa had come to our very good girl
and we watched and we played
and we read and we made

two good days later
with the magic dust settled
I asked what was her favourite
there was no hesitation

Santa had brought her a miniature solar system
the planets, the sun and the moon
all in a box, with paints for the land
the water, the rings

her favourite, but
it lay untouched and discarded
unopened, forgotten
I asked with my eyes and

she laughed as a daughter
can laugh at her father
"I am saving it dad"
she called it the universe

Speaking in Tongues

I know a fireman and asked him
if a burning building contained
a person known
to be evil
to have done despicable things
would he work as hard
risk as much
to douse the flames

he looked at me
from under arched eyebrows
as if I were the bad guy
for considering
even for a moment
the hypothetical answer
to that hypothetical question
or rather, I should say
almost hypothetical

as, given the chance
I would drag my heels
at the sound of the alarm
cling more tightly than usual
on my slide down the pole
I would blare the siren
but not too loud
so as not to wake dozing, nightshift nurses
or startle cooing babies

I would drive safely
taking no chances
clamber from the engine
on sure and steady feet
having felt before the sting
of skinned shins

holding the hose

I would gaze
through rippling air
heavy with ash
at those cleansing orange tongues
greedily doing their work

standing in swirling heat
in symphonies of crackling
popping
sizzling
yet, I am the bad guy
he lowers his eyebrows
he smiles
knowingly
I am joking, of course
I return his smile
and we laugh
and are friends once again
I am joking
of course

Everything Is Invisible

We walked under gothic arches
along the close, tilting streets
of a city, strange to us
we, consciously ignored
by heavy lashed eyes
in sallow faces

we, hopeful holidaying ghosts
clinging to the romance
that rotted around us

slowly, we recognised
the privilege
of being invisible
Barcelona became our playground
with glow stick necklaces
we danced in warm rain
in warm thunder
under warm lightning

we sung in the elevator
laughed in shrieks
on the steps of the cathedral
only then
did they see us
ghosts

when they themselves
had been forgotten

Perfect Nothing

I could hear the smile in his voice on the line
"I'm sorry sir, the payment has been declined."
he didn't sound that sorry
I had hoped to pay the home insurance
to insure us from fire
and theft and
acts of God

instead I drove to the bank and stood in line
somebody was coughing
a dog was barking in the distance
we shuffled along in our line
the world outside

the teller had a glint in his eye
and a crocodile smile and so
I hated him immediately
he couldn't explain the problem with our account
said things instead like, "Never in all my days…"
and, "This is a new one on me Steve, a new one on me."
he knew my name from his computer screen
and used it, like a weapon
I never caught his

I returned home and called again to pay the home insurance
"I'm sorry sir, the payment has been declined."
of course
I asked him to try again
he told me it was a waste of time
I insisted
the payment went through
sometimes pathetic victories are the most precious

I collected my daughter from school
imagine her, taller than ever and curls made for sunshine
my blood reddened
then

she told me her first big lie
I gave her a chance to tell the truth
she held her ground
I gave her another chance
she laid another lie on top
I gave her one final chance
she called my bluff with a tearful promise
I saw my hand shake on the steering wheel

silence
another final chance
she crumbles
takes it
and we try to move on but I feel it
scar tissue, fresh, just inside my ribcage
she is human after all

I wish the day away like a child
I think of sleeping
and waking
into tomorrow, a day of perfect nothing
of turning the music up loud
sitting at the laptop and letting the words come
travelling outside and inside myself

today is not over
but it has gone
parts of it taken by the rivers and streams
more parts taken by the gutter
to the shores and the sewer

Boots

We time travelled today
we downloaded an app that showed
how she will look when she is old
how I will look when I am older

I saw old lines deepen
new lines appear
I saw my hair grey and thin
my eyes sag and dim

we laughed
she called me "granddad"
I imagined, smiling
granddad

she went next
I took her photo, perfect
seven years-old, forever
the sun inside her

we pressed the button
waited
waited
and there she was

old, her life almost lived
old, a mother, maybe
old, a grandmother, maybe
old, without us, definitely

I looked at her, entranced
weary, still beautiful, still herself
but weary
my lines, now her lines

I wondered, I hoped
I worried, how she had earned those lines

I stared into her eyes
I hoped I hadn't failed her

"Let's try Boots next!"
our cat, patient, oblivious
looked the same before, and after
and didn't care

The Oldest Man That Ever Lived

Jiroemon Kimura died at 116 years-old
I need longer
125 should do it
I have to live long enough
for you

I will watch over you
when you walk down autumn streets
strewn with shadows
in the small hours

I will comfort you
when love scalds
and hate burns
I will hold you
surround you with lullabies
as I do now

when, soothing your own daughter
you are distracted
about to step into traffic
I will grab your arm

when sleep won't come
when you need to talk
about everything and nothing
I will be a phone call away

at your retirement party
when the talk is small
and your smile is tired
I will be in the lobby
holding my car keys

if you need help with a tire swing
with anything
for your child

my grandchild
I will be there, tools in hand

I will watch your hair turn
like the seasons
gold to auburn to grey
to white

I will help you climb the steps
when your joints ache
I will nurse you through
the curse of time
I will brush your hair
keep you safe and warm
until

I need to live longer
than Jiroemon Kimura
because no one
will ever love you
as well I as I do

Half Eaten Cookies and Carrots

Like a lot of things, the mint chocolate cheesecake flatters to deceive
it lies in our stomachs, heavy, slowing us down
another Christmas dinner over with
that familiar anti-climactic lethargy

dark fingers tug at our eyelids with the temptation of an afternoon sleep
a once-a-year decadence
but it is brushed aside by the bouncing, giddy thoughts of our daughter
still drunk on the shimmering mystery of half eaten cookies and carrots

we climb into the car
loaded with presents and carols and laughter
and drive into the ever-falling evening
marvelling at the empty streets, the quiet roads

we drive into my Christmas past
my parents just the same but older, smaller, wiser
with half smiles we exchange you-shouldn't-haves
before her little eyes grow heavy

goodbyes are hugged and she sags against my chest
I look at her bundled into her car seat
fading with every passing streetlight
as we drive toward the Christmases to come

Wrapping

I creak my way to the kitchen
noticing the white, winter sun
groggy too
through foggy windows

on the island teeters a tower
Christmas presents with a note
“can you wrap these please?”

still in my morning daze I slowly find
scissors, Sellotape and wrapping paper
I turn on some music to occupy my mind
and watch my hands do their work
measuring, cutting, taping

there is a therapy to it all
the cutting, the sticking, the giving
I imagine the recipient tearing at the paper
curious minds, hurried fingers

of course, there are some
not wrapped with love
I measure out the bare amount
fold a little spite inside
tape a strip of anger down
seal the card with a lick of venom

this is unhealthy and I vow
not to do the same next year
but the morning mist is yet to lift
and I know
there is more poison in me

Just Like That

He tells me that he hasn't enjoyed his life
he is 60 years-old
I have known him ten years
he is a genius
at finding a negative in every positive
time spent in his company is sitting
legs dangling
on the edge of a black hole

I tell him that he still has time to turn it around
he looks at me with burning disdain
he brings his face close to mine
I hold my breath so as not to breathe in his
as spittle
furious and plenty
miniature meteorites
land on my cheek and upper lip
I get the feeling that it was not the response he was looking for

my mother is 80 today
she took me in when I was new
and unwanted
she became my mother
I became her son
just like that

the days would descend into softness
soft light, soft voices, soft words
I would wrap the curtains around myself
disappearing, I would stand
gazing up and half in dreams already
at the soft, flickering light from the television on the ceiling
she would tell me to get ready for bed
I would ask, with stopped heart, for five more minutes
and feel her smile in the pause
sometimes I got ten

now, eight decades in, she tells me
that she is still learning
that she feels stronger now
that sometimes it is hard
I watch her blow out her birthday candles
her face young again for one startling moment
before the flames extinguish

later, we are alone in the sitting room
the curtains long since gone and light, dances for us in the window
she tells me that she agrees with me now
that there is no such thing as heaven
and just like that
I know that we are wrong

The Sigh

"What's wrong? There must be something wrong…"
I knew you would be sceptical when I say
"It was just a sigh."
you are worried, you push
I snap
"It was just a sigh."

I fall, trundling back through time
to find us sitting, hidden, at the back of the bus
on the way to Carlow, our first trip away
being driven towards something
somethings
and it was small, your sigh, as you looked at me and saw
someone else
someone better
someone I could yet become
at your side

I hold her tiny form, new and jaundiced and warm with life
I feel her long, wet sigh
maybe her first
in the crook of my arm
and watch a carpet of goose bumps roll down my skin

I think of him in the hardest of ways
in the now
and the then
when, on a yellow day in Skerries
he gave in to my pleas
and joined me on The Waltzer
just once
my shrieks as we spin and we spin
the clenching of his hands and his teeth and his stomach
and his afterward, never-again, sigh and

I can already see you shake your head
exasperated

sighing through your half smile
when you eventually turn the cushions
to find the stain
I had hoped you never would

Chinaski

you ask me again
"What's wrong?"
but I can't explain
that sometimes I take a gulp of air
and let it out
just because I can
I imagine him at the end of his life
old as sin
covered in cat hair
the room stained with red wine, beer, cigarette ash
and his own self
bent over the typewriter
a human question mark
with all the answers
hammering the keys
at the beginning of night
while the sun burned in him
and keeps burning still

Epsom Salts

My father spoke of Epsom Salts in an almost hush
his own father had bathed in them after a hard day's work
I didn't know whether Epsom was a mineral, a place
or something else
but I did know that it was an elixir
to be spoken of with reverence

years later I played football with men ten and fifteen years older
than me
we fought little wars on big pitches all across Dublin and
afterward
these men, hard and real, spoke solemnly, of Epsom Salts

yesterday evening I played tennis
a sport without contact, full of grace and elegance
against a younger man, a real tennis player, and lost
but there was winning in the losing

I lay in bed an old man
my rotten apple joints burning softly
sleep came as broken glass and nettle stings
and I woke, tired and aching

my wife rang at lunchtime and suggested Epsom Salts
all of a sudden, I was a man
like all the others
a man who needed Epsom Salts

I sunk into the bath and breathed deeply
taking the cure as steam deep into the centre of me
and waited

I thought of all those men and me
older now than they were then
how some have gone and some are going
and how I am tired from just a game of tennis
and maybe other things

Another Storm

I don't remember there being so many storms
I don't remember yellow, orange, red warnings
autumn colours
summer storms

I don't remember there being so many storms
that we have to name them
to differentiate
from once a year to once a month

I don't remember sitting in the small of April
watching the world bend and bleed through windows
thick with rain
feeling our home strain
listening to the furious wind
whistling and whistling
a haunted kettle
something breaks outside
it can wait
something breaks inside

I don't remember there being so many storms

Colombia

I lost my phone today
it took me twenty-five minutes to find it
a twenty-five-minute preview
of old age
of older age

I checked the usual places
twice
before looking, with a sigh
behind the couch, where
under cushions
I found some coins
riches, once upon a time

I looked in the bathroom
still hazy with perfumed steam
scattered with unicorn towels
and broken mermaids

I checked outside, along the wall
beneath our impatient garden clock
that always runs too fast

I checked the shed
disturbing dozing dust motes
for nothing

I checked the treehouse and was met
by the disaffected eyes
of forgotten, plotting dolls

I searched for it
everywhere
but found only resignation

I stood by the coffee machine
listening to its whir

my eyes closed
my mind clear
breathing deeply in
rich aromas all the way from Colombia
I wondered who had harvested the beans
I wondered what they were doing at that moment
I wondered, hypnotised
forgetting about the phone
forgetting about everything
before it was found
just where I had left it

Women Waiting for the Fishermen, Nazaré Beach, Portugal, 1955

The week has ended and we wait
dressed in black
white eyes straining
eager for an imperfection on the horizon

we are not sisters in blood but sisters in waiting
sisters that wait on lemon sand
under an innocent blue sky
sisters that are grey and silent, grey and silent

some pace the beach leaving solitary sets of footprints behind
patterns, broken spirals
serrated waves in the sand waiting themselves
to be smoothed by the greedy ocean

some stand still, unblinking, rosary beads clenched
in lonely, aging hands
some of us have children waiting at home
waiting to be fed

two of us sisters stayed at home today
they still wear black
I see them at the market
they always look away

The Sound of Footsteps in Barcelona

On the Monday we walked 20 kilometres
on the Tuesday we walked 25
driven forward by our hunger to see colours
colours we had seen before
but not like this
not here
in these arrangements
brave and dazzling and everywhere

we walked through aromas thick enough to taste
we swooned at the unexpected romance of the language
we walked and we walked and we walked
under watching gargoyles and cathedral spires
swirls of coloured ice-cream scratching the blue
marvels of architecture

unlike my ankle, the shattered joint rebuilt
with broken jigsaw pieces
that leads to pain clawing its way to the knee above
to the hip above that
to a slipped disc
to Wednesday night and to this bath

I lie chin deep in water
hot as I can take it
I stare at the flickering, Morse code mirror light and now
I understand

Honeyed Breaths

Our summers come in pieces
are gathered to our chests to savour
as we suck in deep, honeyed breaths and revel
in the novelty of squinting

the grass is soft and new beneath our bellies
our faces close, she calls it polished
we search for insects
she talks in pink skinned whispers

I remind her how lucky we are
to have miles of sky above us
and miles of earth below
she nods, she knows

she puts her hand on my back
and for one half-second I am so happy
that I wonder
if I am really here at all

From There To This

There was a beginning
there was a bang, big and loud
and nobody to hear it

there were a series of impossible coincidences
when worlds were born, trembling
when light and dark collided
when the air itself held its breath
a beginning

I drive to buy some milk
over dirt roads and humpback bridges
in a car as beat as I am
one of the rear lights is broken and covered
with part of a Lucozade bottle

from there

to this

The Ghost of Morning

I woke up last night in my childhood
you were there
you all were there
under chirping skies, young again
and lit by impossible sunlight

I lay, tucked away in bed
tucked away in those days
a flickering part of me aware
of the ghost of morning, looming
a beginning
an end

it came of course, this time
in the slow, cautious creak of the bedroom door
in her careful, padding footsteps
in her giddy whisper
"Are you awake yet Dad?"

I opened one eye and she laughed
she opened the curtains and the sun was a needle
poking at me
and the sky was waiting
a beginning
an end

Style
Content

I have many hates
pet
and otherwise
I hate drivers who drive
tooclosebehindme

I hate seeing someone casually
throwing
litter
to
the
ground
I hate reality television, every
genre
of reality television
but
above
/below them
all
I hate poems written with ridiculous
gimmicky
formatting

Grass

Years ago
that expanse of grass
was ripe and waiting
for me
for all of us

now it is something
I need to cross
to get to someplace else
the solicitor
the shop
the bank
the carpark

there I was
here I am

the grass is soft and shiny in the light
a green lake
in which to swim

or drown
smiling

Maynooth, County Kildare

It had not snowed but it was cold enough
that a cobweb might shatter in the wind

he sat there in a derelict porch
calling out in a pained
almost whimpering voice

he was homeless
he was hungry
younger than me
his cheekbones were sharp and pronounced
hair grew in patches on his face
somehow, he didn't shiver as I did
as if his body was half resigned

I brought him sausage rolls
a cup of coffee
and handed him a fiver
he took them in his grey hands
looked at them
with disdain
and asked for twenty

Tea

I pour the milk without stirring
it disappears before returning
blooming
to the surface
and reassurance blooms in me
I learn, once again
that some things do not change
I am reminded that I can be happy
with small things

Mother's Day

The hour sprung forward last night and so
we lose an hour
or gain an hour
I don't know
I never know
I wake up
when I wake up
and the day feels the same

it is Mother's Day
I visit mine, my wife visits hers
I crank up the music as I drive the hour
I have brought her books and flowers
a card with my love in writing
and my daughter's love in doodles
yet we eat together in air that is slightly strained
with the weight of mysterious expectation

hours pass and I find myself driving toward the sun
huge and melting
and I crank up the music again
I stop to shop and carry four large bags of groceries to the car
remembering how she used to do the same
in the days of short trousers
and long laughter

I return home
unload the shopping
empty the dryer
fold the clothes
kiss my daughter's sleepy smile and close her bedroom door
behind me
softly
we make some tea and compare Mother's Days
I yawn
my wife shakes her head ruefully
"That's the extra hour", she says

and I gulp down a question
as to me
it was just a yawn

Like a Moth to a Drain

She does not laugh
she guffaws
oversized tombstones
in her graveyard mouth

suckling monied teat
with vampiric compulsion
she bloats herself
and herself alone

demanding, demeaning, domineering
a wolf in wolf's clothing
a bully, never wrong
never right

tiny demons skate
on the ice in her veins
acid hides
in the corners of her smile

one day, I said, "no more"
my resolve held
just long enough and
I was free

Time does heal
as, with time
Care's depths
are shallowed

Toothache

I lie in bed at 2 a.m.
eyes wide open
seeing nothing
not a flicker of sleep behind them

the toothache does not throb
but is a constant
a tireless hum of ice and metal
that seems to slow down time

night-time thoughts arrive
unwelcome
I remember how my mother told me
to switch them off

she said to reach above
to imagine a switch
to flick it
that all thoughts would scatter

3 a.m. has come and gone
I find myself reaching up
slipping my hand into the darkness
finding an invisible switch, flicking it off

along comes laughter
drowning out my beating heart
in sneering chorus
it seems that I cannot fool myself

the ache has burrowed deeper now
into my jaw
into my ear
give me heartache any day

on bare feet I pad along the hall
my legs steady, the tiredness not yet having reached them

hiding behind my hand I turn on the kitchen lights
and open the press beside the fridge

in amongst the creams and salves
I find someone painkillers
fast acting they say
I hope so

I see a drawing on the fridge door
it is a person with a heart face
with heart arms and heart legs
with heart feet and heart eyes
I remember drawing something similar
when I was her age
when teeth wobbled and fell out painlessly
to be placed under pillows

Rainbow-Tentacled Octopus

From the bus window I would watch them
setting up under high blue skies
a travelling fairground
that, somehow, they squeezed onto a patch of land
it was just the two of them
as old then
as I am now

I saw her throw her head back once
and send her laugh skyward
a happy missile
he looked around sheepishly
a quiet man, smiling

I saw them carry pieces of fantasy from the back of a trailer
I saw him build
I saw her polish
I saw a giant, rainbow-tentacled octopus ready to twirl and rise
and fall
I saw little rockets ready to scrape the edge of the sky
I saw a house of mirrors reflecting ever greying hair

days and weeks and months slipped idly by
and worse still
I let them
before realising that summers were passing
and the patch of land remained empty
but of course, children find other things to do
and I saw other things out the bus window
some years later we moved and, not far from us, I saw the rides
again
they sat on a small patch of land beside a mobile home
there were the rockets
there were the waltzers
there were the bumper cars
there was the carousel covered with stars and cartoon hearts
and there was he

sitting on a white plastic chair
looking at them

he was there most days
melting slowly into his plastic chair
he was alone now
and sat in his garish fairground graveyard
looking at fading octopus tentacles
now still

one sunny day, I was walking past him
for the first time in all these years I spoke to him
just, “hello”
he nodded me a smile
always the quiet man
in another life it was a fairground day
but in this life, I was close enough to see the paint cracking
on the carousel cartoon hearts

The Summer of the Rabbit

We looked everywhere
for our disappeared rabbit
hunched over, we paced the garden
calling out her name as if she might answer
we looked inside too as sometimes
she ventured indoors and sat
in perfect contentment
beneath the kitchen table

your face pale, you suggested we check outside
beyond our garden walls
the infinite land of cars and voices
we walk
calling
every step more fraught with worry
heads down we walk
and search
but all we find are lengthening shadows
until night falls
bringing with it
dread and heavy certainty

in bed you tell me that you realise
it is only a rabbit
though the words catch in your throat
a new day comes
and another
I see you gaze out the kitchen window
the hope leaving you in salty trails on your cheeks
summer comes to save you
you talk of our rabbit in the past tense
I think it is over

under autumn skies I try to remove the leaves
from the little gap between the shed and the wall
before my rake catches something on its way out
something inert

not alive
once alive
I see my breath hang in the air before me

I eventually manage to dislodge the rabbit
it is dead
of course
but its coat is still lustrous
its little tail still, as if between twitches, still so soft
after all this time, it is perfect
a stuffed toy
a stuffed toy
with its head perfectly cleaved off
as if by a surgeon
there is no blood
I put it in a black plastic bag and into the bin
among used teabags and empty milk cartons

this is what minks do
they remove and devour and drain
and leave you gazing out the kitchen window on summer days

Days and Nights and Nights and Days

I don't know where it comes from
I don't know where it goes
but long before I see it
I can feel it

it slips between the laughter
it shoots between the stars
and the moon-white of its eyes reminds me
that night will fall on the sunniest day

The Roller Disco

I held my daughter's hand as we stumble-skated
long circles of hearts stopping and hearts racing
exchanging eyes-to-heaven glances with another father

it was almost empty and the music echoed
besides us, there were a group of girls
slurping blue slushies and chattering in gasps

then, I saw another teenage girl
alone and heavy
she must have weighed fifteen stone, maybe more

she put on her skates clumsily
with dimpled knuckles
we skated on

"look at her"
said my daughter
pointing

I turned around with dread
and saw her
weightless

gliding, easily
as if pulled along
by a thousand fairies

we watched as she twirled
like water down a sink
and smiled at my daughter

while skating backwards as she passed
skipping from one foot
to the other

I saw my little girl inch taller

comforted by the knowledge
that impossible is just a word

that life is hers
and ripe for plucking
she lets go of my hand

time stretches and contracts
in that peculiar way
and we watch her

heavy and light
fifteen stone of song
swaying and swooping and

she falls
corners of her landing hard
marrow freezing in my bones

there is a sound then
vicious snorts
sneering laughter

the group of girls
slushies gone
white teeth, pointing

I want to run to them
to scream into their faces
until my throat is raw

I want to pull their tongues
from their mouths
and stamp them to a paste

instead, we help her up
she feels light still
in my arms

my daughter takes my hand
I see the beginnings of tears
as she is not too young to realise

we take off our skates
and put on our shoes
and get the hell out of there

Concrete

Maybe Leonard Cohen had it backward
maybe the cracks are where the light leaks out
there is a dog barking in the distance
if he barks on a sunny day
I imagine him bounding, basking, glowing
if the day is miserable
those same barks are lonesome
an oddly infectious sorrow

today the clouds are low and flat and grey
concrete
perfectly laid
no cracks at all
they do not move
they just hang there
bouncing back those barks
this was supposed to be a happy poem

Humming Bird
For Robin

We woke as enemies today
the three of us
a day of possibilities
of crisp blue and straight roads

we sniped and snapped
glared and glowered
and let those hours fall
to shatter at our feet

words were barbed
questions acid tinged
smiles perfunctory
through closed lips

the night drive home was quiet
we enemies, tired
in a halfway trance
our pupils pulsing
with the passing street lights

defeated by ourselves
we craved our sleep
dreamt of dreams
before

from the backseat
a hum
gentle at first
but slowly building
and then my head is bobbing
and my foot is tapping
and we are humming together
we three enemies a chorus
in perfectly imperfect harmony
and fifteen minutes later

we turn onto our driveway
throats raw
hearts full
and the night ours for the taking

Birdsong

It might the song of the lark
the blackbird, the nightingale
but on this spring evening there is birdsong
rushing toward the corners of the sky

there are no distant cars
no lawnmowers
no children squealing
the world is bowed in reverence

the crow looks on
biding its time
holding back its song of rusted razors
until the symphony reaches its apex and

his squawk, sudden and flat
scatters them in silhouette
across the laughing sun

Pure and Infinite

We talked about the snow today
the snow that slept it out
and startled buds and blooms
blanketing spring instead

how we played in the fluffy deep
in that soft and hungry quiet
how we were not trapped, but free
and how, it will not return
until she is a mother too

the still new whites of her eyes
pure and infinite as that snow
cannot leap forward as mine can
to when youth has flown from her
and landed somewhere else

Purple Fingers Broken Nails

1
The first day of school
tears hot on my cheeks
summer is over

don't make me grow up
take me home
where the radio aerial
glints in the kitchen
just take me home

2
In plenty of time
I pull on the brakes
my stomach a knot
at the sound of their snap
I cling to my handlebars
your voice chasing me

terror is born
clouding my mind
the hill pulls me downward
I hear the limp
in your footsteps
falling behind me

railings punish
my indecision

remorselessly

you carry me to the car
I cannot stop staring
at my purpled fingers
at my broken nails

blood pulses from knuckles

take me home
take me home
take me home

3
Falling in love
not at first sight
at second
your eyes lit
by coloured
broken glass bottles
I catch your words in my hands
stuff them into my pockets
take me home
oh, take me home

4
Losing so many
so many to go
I have learned that the dead
do not leave
empty handed

after all

take me home
to unsinging birds
take me home

5
I will be betrayed
by pieces of myself
the grass
eternal, damp with dew

take me home
return me
to the soil
take me home

Heels First

It was one of those forever days
days put aside for children and
where now stand regimented houses
once stood hay, swaying deliriously
unaware
that every summer has an ending

they were just shapes at first, rippling
and smaller than a fingernail
we had heard stories of these boys
older, tougher, dangerous
and cowardice, hidden in the yellow
hungrily rose up through us

we crept behind our hay mountain
hatching plans with wide eyes and nodding heads
then burrowed, one by one, inside
hidden in saccharin darkness
silent besides our heartbeats
loud as thunder in our ears

time did not fly then
it crashed and it burned
and we lay in its wreckage
waiting
and waiting
and then

voices, seeped toward us, chilling us
through gritted teeth we prayed
and swore our offertories
but, they did not walk on by
and their voices became laughter
laughter dark as oil

they climbed upon our hay mountain
pretending not to know

that beneath them, we lay, prone
and they pretended not to know
that their heels sharpened
with each and every jump

there might still be a someday
where we erupt
from the bowels of our mountain
effortlessly razing them
but, that day, we took our punishment
in silence

and the field
now a mass of houses
concrete worlds in miniature
concrete
on our childhood

Quiet Embers

Head lowered I walked over and over
through the rain
into wind
I saw blurring newspapers
melt into the ground

I flung myself at the feet of a sculptress
for long years
to be chiselled
away from myself

inside, quiet embers
sparked to fire
as I
returned
each day
to you

Dad

unprepared for winter's attack
he was left shivering
his armour stripped from him
lost, he looks for cotton in the snow
and I watch
helplessly
a glass pane of pride between us

I follow
as I have always done
once, I followed him through blacks and whites
a compass in his stomach
obsidian eyes blazing
I follow now
through greys
collecting armfuls of his memories
delicate as cobwebs
as they fall from him
in the gentlest of breezes

School Gate

Waiting at the school gate I realise
I have perfected something
I have perfected the art of not catching eyes
with anyone
but her

I stand there, safe, on another continent
where the sun shines
where there is silence in the chatter
idle gossip can stay idle
while I wait, content
among others, alone

once in a while someone steps into my bubble
we engage in small talk
minute talk
microscopic talk
the weather
the weekend
the weather

I am apart
perhaps aloof
until she emerges
bouncing yellow curls
searching blue eyes
find mine and I have missed her and I feel my mouth turn upward
and, you know
there is nothing like it

One For Sorrow
For John Martyn

I found you beneath the bridge near the docks
you were missing your right leg at the knee
there were other parts missing too
under your sprawling frame
the wheelchair looked ready to fall asunder
a guitar lay across you, held, delicately
by your bloated hands, powder white, almost ghostly

I had been rushing for a bus when we caught eyes
I hadn't meant to stop but then
you pressed the veins of your guitar
and my blood ran cold
impossible music, it was impossible
those angled, swirling notes
strums that thumped me in the chest
your fingers heavy, light, so light, bumblebees

we caught eyes again and you broke my heart
you smiled and broke my heart
I knew it all then, somehow
I saw the calendar pages piling on the floor
I felt the loneliness dulled by whiskey
I saw your baby boy twinkling in your hands
I felt the sting of the needles and
the blessed relief

you closed your eyes then
eyes lost in your swollen face and
opened your mouth and your voice
rising up from your stomach
released as shards into the night
every word a hardship
each line disintegrating with cracks and embers
I saw your fists hit her
I saw the blood on your knuckles
I heard the laughter when you tried to stand

and fell, far from home
you escaped yourself, eventually
I knew that soon
you would escape it all
you broke my heart

afterward we talked
though there was nothing left to say
the static in our handshake brought one last smile
and I left you
changed
I ran into the rest of my life
I ran as fast as I could but I knew
I knew that if I caught that bus it would not honour you
it would cheapen it all but
I had to try

trying to catch up on time I ran
feeling the wind cool the tears on my cheeks
my chest burning
my legs shaking, screaming

I saw the lights
soft and red and distant on the Ha'penny Bridge
I ran and ran, away from you until
I was close enough to touch it
close enough to look up and see myself
on any other day and then
the bus pulled into the dampening evening

Stings and Swings

Children can be so cruel

I didn't know what that meant
not really
until I left childhood behind

there are sneers and sniffles on the wind
as I walk toward the schoolyard
I watch them gathered in bunches
chattering birds

I see one little boy mocking his classmate
he is relentless
she is autistic
he is relentless
she breaks
she cries open mouthed yet
in silence
huge tears bloom
large enough to roll down her flushed cheeks
over her quivering jaw
down her neck
to where they soak into her collar
he walks away
he has won

another boy is crying in gulps
his knee bloody
damp rust on a hinge
a girl asks him if he is okay
I hear him shout that he doesn't need help
from a girl

I hear a conversation
"you are wrong!"
"no, you are wrong!"
"I am not wrong, you are!"

“you are so wrong!”
so many wrongs

one little girl stands amongst it all
knee deep in it all
and looks through it all
she smiles
and runs to me
not knowing that I was cruel once

Fighting In An Empty House

Let's face it, she was a bitch
though she took no joy in it
it was how she was built

joy for her was a cloth
wrung and wrung and always dry

maybe that's why we stuck around
why we kept returning
why we kept calling to hear her voice
sharp and abrasive on the other end of the line
she was blameless
we smelled roses
she felt thorns

life, for her, was endured and now
at her wake
we share stories and laugh with strangers
old, old friends
childhood neighbours lost to time
newly found

she suffered us, we suffered her
we steeled ourselves for her barbs
her vehemence, her insolence
we ran out of patience but we were stubborn
she would not defeat us
we loved her

she spent a lifetime pushing us away
all of us, yet
here we are
together, despite her, tearily reminiscing
she would have hated it
she would have loved it too

Red

I was a boy, playing alone on the road outside my house
my ball got away from me and I turned to chase it
I saw another boy, not much older than myself, jump over his garden wall and run across the road
toward a park filled with other children, happy sounds
he ran, he did not look, he ran
the driver could do nothing
the boy ran right under the wheels
I remember no sound and no colour besides the grey of the road and red
so much red
it was as if he had burst
I ran inside to tell my mother what I had seen
I don't remember being upset
I just remember telling her
she did not believe me
I went back outside with my ball under my arm
I remember seeing blood, shiny and bright running toward the kerb and pooling there
I remember wondering if it would leave a stain

Calendars

1

School over
we come home and
our house strains
to hold our laughter

2

With her friends
she will come home
to fill her room
with excited whispers

3

In the small hours
she will come home, tiptoeing
and we will finally
fall asleep

4

With her love
she will come home, shy and proud
and there will be small talk
over dinner

5

School over
she will go home and
her house will strain
to hold their laughter

6

In time
she will come home
and
tea poured
we will smile
and reminisce

Albufeira Breezes

Around and around she goes under the low, low sun
all milk teeth and excited trembles
we watch her, perched on the miniature quad bike
lemon curls, sea blue eyes

she whizzes around the marbled beachfront square
zigzagging through a procession of other children
an old-fashioned bugle is fixed to the handlebars
she is the only one that uses it
“this is so dangerous daddy!”
“I will go even faster next time!”
“are you watching mammy?”

Albufeira breezes take her joy and carry it out to sea
to surprised fishermen and expectant mermaids
and around and around she goes and
under the low, low sun, we wait
and I realise
everything is waiting
after all

Toothpaste

The bedroom door burst open and I felt that sudden pulse
adrenaline, that half second of panicked limbo
then, I saw your eyes, full of sparks, and I relaxed
you thrust your little fist toward me
unfurling, slowly, the reveal of a sorceress and
in your palm, an empty toothpaste cap

that little stab as I looked at you with questions
and you, filled with gentle, mocking disappointment
pointed into the cap and I saw some toothpaste residue
that familiar blue and white
you told me to look again, to *really* look, and so I did

you explained, patiently, that inside the cap
the toothpaste leaves a pattern and
looking again I saw a perfect swirl of colour, pulled into a point
an unnoticed everyday masterpiece
I looked back to you and we smiled
comforted in shared understanding

you told me that it was the best one yet
the "yet" bringing a thunderous wave of reassurance
as I glimpsed into your future
and saw it filled with wonder

The Grass

Cloudless skies resting on dusty terracotta cliffs
bring needles of envy to my browning skin
as I imagine driving to work each day, surrounded

I imagine running late while staring, ravenously
at the jewel-filled ocean and rippling, cresting hills

repeatedly and madly, I fall in love with every smile
all the more dazzling when set in sallow skin

yet now, just ten days here, in paradise
I am looking straight ahead while walking
those mighty cliffs somehow less worthy of my reverence
and when a Portuguese girl
asks, if the grass, coarse here, is the same in Ireland
I realise
that it is not

Chasing Geckos

We lost her today
not for moments
not for seconds
but for minutes
for lifetimes

we were adventurers
searching for geckos
hearing rustles
seeing grass spring back
and leaves tremble

she went one way
we went another
trees mumbling between us
twenty seconds later
where we should have met
she was gone
we were there
and she, was gone

gentle calls unanswered
we heard rustles
saw grass spring back
and leaves tremble
so much sunshine
so much shadow
our calls grew louder
our calls were panicked
our voices cracked
and we were running
and there was no answer
and she, was gone

I thought of endings
of suns, falling bloodied into the sea
of finding, in ten years' time

her toys
in the attic

then, her distant squeal
behind a scrambling gecko
and my knees turned to water
and life began again

This Eden

A few weeks have passed us sumptuously by
and we are wallowing happily here in this Eden
where geckos roam in place of snakes
where evenings are the sun, buttered
across pinks and fading blues
where ocean spray is welcomed on our browning skin

yet, I miss rich greens, and early morning fog
I miss the earnest music of distant lawnmowers
the perfect crackle of my parents' analogue radio
I miss our home, our bed a hand, catching me
our sally tree, wise and heavy with wet leaves
Ireland
beautiful
without us

A Conversation with My Daughter

She stood on the balcony, the whole of Portugal behind her
the whirling shrieks of her friends below her
the surround of the pool speckled with water
evidence of belly flops and cannonballs

she stood on the balcony, the curving Atlantic horizon behind her
coves and cliffs, pools and piers to be explored
sandcastles eager to be built
seashells waiting patiently to be found

she stood on the balcony, facing me
"Dad, I just had ideas for two comics. Would you like to know what they are?"
"Yep."
"Okay, the first comic is going to be about a bold cat who steals kids and then forces them to make furniture from their own sweat."
"Good God, okay, what is the second comic going to be about?"
"Elbows."

she stood on the balcony, facing me
the whole world behind her
and I realised
this is love

The Sun on Our Backs

And so, here it comes, an ending
real life waits on the other side
a good life, a great life
so much to return to but
so much to leave
I make impossible wishes
and find myself wanting to stop time
to ridiculously, literally, actually stop time

just for us
that little while longer
all the sweeter for being ours and ours alone
I dream of freezing time while our crepes cook
so that we may run our hands through their warm aromas
inhaling them just one last time

I dream of freezing time under that churning bloody moon
so that we may beat our chests and
send joyous howls towards it
I dream of freezing time through will alone
whilst the troubadour sings and strums and she dances
taking great gulps of music into her marrow, she dances

I beg to freeze time just a second before that lady
in easy holiday conversation, lets slip that she was happier
a decade ago, before her son was born
just a second before that father tells me of his brother's suicide
three New Year's Eve's previous

I wish and I beg and I yearn and I ache but time
is a cat
walking along the keys of an old piano

Home

Yes, there were tears, plump and twinkling in those last sun rays
the subdued airport drive and goodbyes to the sea and the sand
the palm trees, still exotic to us
as we left them behind
one more chance to use our pidgin Portuguese
then we, cheating evolution, were airborne

above the clouds, the world below
a film set, intricate, quaint
to which we soon would return
in the muffled cabin air, I feel, more than hear
a sound at my shoulder
my smiling daughter, crying at the rolling green
"we are home"

we are corralled, dishevelled, into sweating Orwellian lines
and unashamedly await our stoic processing
we shuffle onward in shared lethargy and then

outside the airport, heaped in bags, we wait
but my father cannot find us and calls, upset
life no longer his for the taming
he has given up and driven home defeated
my heart chokes
we hail a taxi

and arrive at my parent's home
a home that bulges with memories

it is my birthday
but in the six weeks, it is they who have aged
somehow smaller, slightly weaker
they had shaken hands with death
twice and nearly three times
while we ate and swam and sung and blazed

I wanted them with us

where all the sea was sky and we
standing on the pier
stood at the edge of the world
I wanted to give them my eyes to see

my father, whose staircase footsteps woke me
in the small of childhood nights
went to bed in twilight, in twilight
on the day of my birth
on the evening we returned to them
followed, soon after by my mother
there is our blue gate
there is our long, hooded driveway
there is our home, our home
there is the key in the lock, turning
there is our hall, our kitchen
there are our beds
there are we, disturbing happy flotsam

that night sleep caught us and took us deep
under dreamless treacle waves
all of us
separate, but
with fewer miles between us

Also Available From
Cajun Mutt Press

Owls in Hot Rods with Pink Elephants and Dead Bats
by James D. Casey IV
ISBN# 1548246220

Haight
by Red Focks
ISBN# 172647125X

Absurd
by R. Bremner
ISBN# 1725983613

Isomorphic
by James D. Casey IV
ISBN# 1724001140

Dark Linings
by Joanne Olivieri
ISBN# 1727550374

Death & Love/Love & Death
by James D. Casey IV
ISBN# 1727853857

Juggernaut Fuzz
by Ryan Quinn Flanagan
ISBN# 1730783333

Also Available From
Cajun Mutt Press

This Many Years After The War
by Matthew Borczon
ISBN# 1731194226

Wild Rose Country
by R. Keith
ISBN# 0578439816

Detritus Of The Drunken Night
by Ian Lewis Copestick
ISBN# 1092511148

Dreams Of Mongolia
by Will Mayo
ISBN# 1093504102

Requiem for a Robot Dog
by Lauren Scharhag
ISBN# 1099369037

Unwritten Words That Slide Down The Wall
by James D. Casey IV
ISBN# 1099516676

Printed in Poland
by Amazon Fulfillment
Poland Sp. z o.o., Wrocław